Praises for
The Real Scandal of the Evangelical Mind

What is the state of the evangelical mind? Carl Trueman intends to re-shape that entire question, and he does so by questioning the very existence of evangelicalism. In this clever book, Trueman forces us all to think about the most basic issues of evangelical identity, integrity, and credibility. This work comes from a first-rate evangelical scholar. Read it at your own risk.

—R. ALBERT MOHLER JR.
President and Joseph Emerson Brown
Professor of Christian Theology
The Southern Baptist Theological Seminary

Professor Trueman offers a clear and sober assessment of contemporary evangelicalism and how its doctrinal neglect as well as its ecclesial and institutional practices continue to sever its intellectual and moral life from its biblical and theological roots. As a Catholic, I part ways with Professor Trueman on several doctrinal questions. But when it comes to our common heritage as Christians—and our shared understanding of the good, the true, and the beautiful—I stand with him against a spirit of the age that will not rest until all the vestiges of Christian civilization are vanquished from the face of the Earth.

What is truly tragic—as Professor Trueman forcefully argues—is that some who claim to be allies of that civilization, as well as friends of all things "evangelical," embrace and propagate ideas that aid and abet its destruction. Although he may not agree with me on this, perhaps it is time for evangelicals (as well as Catholics) to consider what Alasdair MacIntyre has called "the Benedict Option."

—FRANCIS J. BECKWITH
Professor of Philosophy and Church-State Studies
Baylor University

THE REAL
scandal of the
EVANGELICAL
mind

Carl R. Trueman

MOODY PUBLISHERS
CHICAGO

© 2011 by
CARL R. TRUEMAN

Edited by Jim Vincent
Interior design: Puckett Smartt
Cover design: Kathryn Joachim
Cover image: iStock Photo © morkeman #716869

ISBN: 978-0-8024-05746

We hope you enjoy this book from Moody Publishers. Our goal is to provide high-quality, thought-provoking books and products that connect truth to your real needs and challenges. For more information on other books and products written and produced from a biblical perspective, go to www.moodypublishers.com or write to:

Moody Publishers
820 N. LaSalle Boulevard
Chicago, IL 60610

9 10 8

Printed in the United States of America

Contents

Acknowledgments

First, I would like to thank Madison Trammel of Moody Publishers for having the idea for this booklet and then commissioning me to write it.

In addition, I am as always indebted to good friends who were willing to read my material in draft form and offer constructive criticism and advice. In this case, both the Rev. Todd Pruitt, senior pastor of Church of the Savior in Wayne, Pennsylvania, and Dr. Mike Reeves, theological advisor to the Universities and Colleges Christian Fellowship (United Kingdom), gave generously of their time and talents. To be able to call on such good pastoral and theological colleagues is truly one of the great joys and blessings of my life; thus, I dedicate this booklet to these two gentlemen in acknowledgment of all the faithful work they do in their respective spheres.

Introduction

It has been some fifteen years since Mark Noll, then a professor of history at Wheaton College, published his famous tract for the times, *The Scandal of the Evangelical Mind*.[1] Writing from the context of a Christian liberal arts college, Noll expressed in the book his frustration at what he saw as evangelicals' intellectual and cultural sterility. For a book that arguably stated the obvious, it made a remarkable impact, with its titular phrase becoming a veritable cliché—a cliché that I am happy to adapt for the title of this essay.

Professor Noll blamed many aspects of evangelicalism for the cultural wasteland he said it had become, prominent among them the American predilection for dispensationalism, with its passive, "pull up the drawbridge and wait for the end of the world" mentality toward general cultural pursuits. (Although, one might note, American dispensationalists have been far from passive in at least one area of cultural engagement: conservative politics.) The other area of intellectual suicide identified by Noll was literal, six-day creationism.

While these two beliefs were in Noll's view symptomatic of the intellectual malaise within evangelicalism, underlying his analysis was a broader conviction that American evangelicalism historically had faced internal opposition to intellectual and cultural engagement. Professor Noll hinted at this same critique in one of his lesser-known books, *Between Faith and Criticism*, where he also offered a somewhat rose-tinted perspective of the British scene. Evangelicals in the United Kingdom modeled a better paradigm for combining faith and learning,[2] he said, whereas American evangelicalism, with its fundamentalist-revivalist-pragmatic roots, had always been inherently anti-intellectual.

Catholic scholar Etienne Gilson's words about Francis of Assisi summarize well Professor Noll's complaint against evangelicalism and its leaders: "It is clear that he never condemned learning for itself, but that he had no desire to see it developed in his Order. In his eyes it was not in itself an evil, but its pursuit appeared to him unnecessary and dangerous. Unnecessary, since a man may save his soul and win others to save theirs without it; dangerous, because it is an endless source of pride."[3]

Such anti-intellectual obscurantism, of which Noll said dispensationalism and six-day creationism were the most obvious manifestations, had made evangelicals a marginal group. Not in the broader culture, of course, where the evangelical vote was politically significant, but rather in those sections of society where ideas were the stock-in-trade, where mainstream intellectual engagement took place. To a professor at Wheaton College, which had long aspired to be the evangelical Harvard, this marginalization was cause for heartbreak and lament.

Fifteen years later, the intellectual and cultural poverty of American evangelicals would seem to continue, even as church attendance is holding up reasonably well in the U.S. (at least in comparison to other industrialized nations). Without making a judgment for or against any of the following positions, I would add these common beliefs of evangelicals to dispensationalism and six-dayism as causes of the movement's social and intellectual marginality: biblical inerrancy, opposition to women's ordination and homosexuality and abortion, religious exclusivism, and rejection of the broad claims of evolutionary science. Commitment to any or all of these positions places one at the fringe of culture, at least of thoughtful, educated culture.

Given the recent onslaught of the so-called new atheism, with its rhetorical arsenal of ridicule and mockery, it would seem that the question of the scandal of the evangelical mind is ripe for revisiting. If Professor Noll feared that the late twentieth century featured a climate where a literal six-day creation and the excesses of dispensationalism were distancing evangelicals from the wider world, what can be said of today? In the wake of the "four horsemen" of atheism—Richard Dawkins, Daniel Dennett, Sam Harris, and Christopher Hitchens—and in the aftermath of 9/11, "fundamentalism" has become a popular bogeyman. The scholarly construct of said fundamentalism has proved elastic enough to extend past the hard-line fanatics of religious movements. Any Muslim who takes his or her religion seriously is liable to be seen as a potential terrorist, however loyal and well-behaved in the civic sphere. Christians who hold to traditional views of the Bible, sin, and the afterlife fall into the same broad category of "fundamentalists," right alongside Osama bin Laden and the Aryan Nation. The times have changed much faster than Professor Noll seemed to anticipate, and for the worse. Indeed, it is clear that from the perspective of wider society, religious beliefs are more scandalous now than they have been for many years.

So does the scandal of the evangelical mind continue? I will argue ahead that it does, though not at all in the manner that Noll maintained. The views of some evangelicals do, indeed, marginalize us in the public square, but that is not the central problem confronting evangelicalism today. More concerning is the lack of any consensus about evangelicalism's intellectual identity—an issue Noll may have noticed in 1994 but that has grown more pronounced in recent years. For there to be a scandal of the evangelical mind, there must be not just a mind, but also a readily identifiable thing called an "evangelical" and a movement called "evangelicalism" —and the existence of such is increasingly in doubt.

NOTES

1. Mark A. Noll, *The Scandal of the Evangelical Mind* (Grand Rapids: Baker, 1994).

2. Mark A. Noll, *Between Faith and Criticism* (Grand Rapids: Baker, 1991).

3. Quoted in James A. Weisheipl, *Friar Thomas D'Aquino* (Washington, D.C.: Catholic University of America, 1983), 65.

CHAPTER ONE

Losing Our Religion?

Is there an evangelical mind active today? Nearly two decades ago Mark Noll concluded any evangelical mind had gone soft through lack of use. Today the question is whether a healthy evangelicalism exists to host such a mind. I am not sure, theologically, that such a thing still thrives.

We may all be victims of language at this point. The adjective "evangelical" appears to refer to something real. Yet as every child finds out on that fateful day when Santa Claus is discovered to be a stage name for Mom or Dad—or, as a trendy postmodern evangelical might say in surely unpretentious and helpful language, "a floating signifier with no extra-textual referentiality, rooted in a communal semiotic scheme designed to maintain an oppressive patriarchy"—words do not always refer to something that exists. "Santa Claus," "unicorns," "Batman," and "drinkable American tea" are all words or phrases that, despite their seeming reality, have no true reference point.

EVANGELICALISM: A REVEALING DEFINITION

"Evangelical" and "evangelicalism" seem to have become similar terms; at the very least, they mean much less now than they appear to mean. Consider the influential definition of evangelicalism offered by David Bebbington. The historian defines the movement with four hallmarks: (1) biblicism (a high regard for the Bible as the primary source of spiritual truth), (2) crucicentrism (a focus on the atoning work of Christ on the cross), (3) conversionism (a belief in the necessity of spiritual conversion), and (4) activism (the priority of publicly proclaiming and living out the gospel). Although many still debate the adequacy of this definition, it does capture the flavor of what has historically been understood by the term "evangelicalism."1

Three aspects of Bebbington's definition are of particular interest: the lack of any institutional or ecclesiastical dimension, the primacy of experience, and the nearly complete absence of doctrinal criteria. As to the first point, if for the sake of argument we grant evangelicalism an existence, then its lack of an ecclesiology highlights that it has always been, for want of a better word, trans-denominational. Thus, like so many other "isms," from Puritanism to socialism, it can be difficult to determine its boundaries. Unlike, say, identifying Catholics, Anabaptists, Methodists, Presbyterians, and Episcopalians, who can be spotted by their church affiliations, determining who are evangelicals is a much trickier and ultimately subjective task.2

Second, the emphasis on experience arguably reinforces the definitional problem—it pushes evangelicalism further away from an ecclesiastical identity and toward mysticism and subjectivity. No doubt many evangelicals would respond with the obvious: Unless you have the experience, you cannot be part of our church; therefore, evangelicalism does have an ecclesiastical dimension. This response, however, merely exacerbates the third problem, the lack of doctrinal criteria for the movement. If church membership is built on an experience, then where does doctrine fit in?

This, arguably, is the primary problem confronting evangelicalism. An emphasis on a defining experience does not mesh comfortably with an emphasis on doctrinal identity. Ultimately, the question of which is more significant, the experience or the doctrine, must be confronted. Like the medieval theologians who wrestled with whether theology was a theoretical or a practical discipline, most self-declared evangelicals would answer that both theology and experience are necessary. Yet that raises the complex question of how much weight is to be placed upon each. In practice, evangelical organizations and institutions typically adopt minimal doctrinal statements; many evangelicals place relatively little weight on a fully conceived theological statement or identity.

REMEMBERING ONE DOCTRINAL DEBATE

Some years ago I attended a meeting of the Association of Theological Schools (ATS), the North American accrediting agency for seminaries. As is typical at such gatherings, a wide variety of schools were represented, from Jewish to Catholic to Eastern Orthodox. At one point during the day we were divided along confessional lines to discuss particular issues facing our institutions. I was in the evangelical group, which included Baptists, Pentecostals, Presbyterians, and free-church people. In my group were two very unalike members—one sympathetic to open theism, a committed radical Arminian whose suspicion of metaphysics made his commitment to the language of Trinitarian and Christological orthodoxy equivocal; the other a straight-down-the-line Westminster Confession Presbyterian, completely comfortable with the so-called five points of Calvinism and the traditional Western formulations of classical theism. Being familiar with the writings of both men, I decided to sit back and enjoy the ensuing fireworks display.

Sure enough, at some point during the vigorous engagement

between these two professors, the Presbyterian commented that he and the radical Arminian really did not have much in common. The Arminian responded to the Presbyterian with some exasperation, "But surely we can agree that we both love Jesus?"

I was tempted to pipe up, "Yes, you both do; it's just a shame you don't agree on who He was or what He did." Instead, I stayed politely silent and allowed my eyes to wander to other areas of the room—to the Catholic group and the Orthodox group, where I realized that, strange to tell, I had more in common with some members of each of those than I did with the radical Arminian.

So why was I in this group? How come he and I were both "evangelicals," and I was thus understood to be closer doctrinally to a virtual open theist than to a traditional, anti-Pelagian Dominican, whose basic doctrine of God would at least be substantially the same as my own?

It appears ATS was operating under an assumed definition of evangelicalism that took minimal account of doctrinal distinctives. It placed in the evangelical group those who were committed in some way to taking the Bible seriously, to evangelism, to the importance of Jesus Christ, and to some kind of existential commitment to God—additionally, those who were not Catholic or Orthodox. My vague qualification of "in some way" is deliberate, pointing to what I believe is a lack of clarity about any kind of hard and fast doctrinal identity for evangelicals. However the ATS viewed its working definition, it seems to have amounted in practice to little more than a judgment based on demographics or aesthetics: Evangelicals presumably look, sound, and act in ways that are unlike Catholics and the Orthodox.

While one might dismiss this grouping as the action of an accreditation body that is simply clueless about evangelicalism, the selection of seminaries and schools for inclusion in the evangelical group was scarcely exceptional. Westminster Seminary in California, Gordon-Conwell Theological Seminary, Trinity Evangelical Divinity School, Baylor University, and Wheaton College were all represented, to name just a few. Such a list could not be considered mainline or Catholic or Orthodox; without question, it would have to be regarded as evangelical, whether or not every member of the group was comfortable with such a designation. This dilemma highlights my basic point, that evangelicalism lacks clear doctrinal definition within the wider Christian community.

GOSPEL PEOPLE?

At this point, some readers might want to respond that evangelicals are, by definition, gospel people. I have a hunch that many Catholics, Orthodox, and liberal mainliners also regard themselves as gospel people. In fact, this designation begs the question of what one means by the word "gospel" and thus cannot advance the discussion very far. Typically, organizations and institutions that regard themselves as evangelical have sought to flesh out their doctrinal identities beyond the Bebbington quadrilateral—biblicism, crucicentrism, conversionism, and activism—and unqualified references to the gospel. The results, however, have often been less than satisfactory, at least in providing a thorough theological definition of what evangelicalism might be.

Thus, the Evangelical Theological Society's statement of faith is forty-three words long and affirms only the Bible's inerrancy in the autographs and the doctrine of the Trinity.[3] If evangelicalism is supposed to be doctrinally distinctive, this statement gives no clue as to what makes an evangelical different from, say, a conservative Roman Catholic, Eastern Orthodox, or Anglo-Catholic believer—all of whom could sign the statement with integrity and without compromise, though most would protest any suggestion that they are evangelical. Indeed, the ETS statement heightens the problem of a definition rather than pointing toward a resolution.

The Alliance of Confessing Evangelicals (which, to be clear about my own leanings, is a group with which I am affiliated) has a faith statement that affirms the five solas of the Reformation: grace alone, faith alone, Scripture alone, Christ alone, and the glory of God alone.[4] This statement is certainly more adequate than that of the ETS; it could not, for example, be signed in good conscience by a Roman Catholic. However, it belongs to a group that is not simply "evangelical" but also "confessing." In other words, the Alliance of Confessing Evangelicals self-consciously presents itself as a distinctive subset of the wider evangelical phenomenon. As such, it offers little help in producing a general doctrinal definition for the movement as a whole.

Indeed, "confessing" is just one among a plethora of adjectives that can be used to qualify evangelicalism, including "open," "Arminian," "Anabaptist," "Lutheran," "Reformed," "conservative," "emergent," and "postmodern," to list but a few. It should become clear, then, that the essence of evangelicalism cannot be defined by any particular view of the sacraments, predestination, atonement, free will, justification, ecclesiology, or even God's knowledge of the future. Seen in this light, the question again raises its awkward head of whether we can speak in any meaningful, doctrinally defined way about evangelicalism as a cohesive movement. The ATS's apparent assumption that an evangelical is anyone who is a Christian, takes the Bible and Jesus seriously, but is not mainline, Catholic, or Orthodox, is arguably as good a definition as we have.

Furthermore, if in practice evangelicalism lacks a doctrinal center beyond taking the Bible and Jesus seriously (in some sense), then even an emphasis on the new birth is insufficient to give it coherence. Experience without doctrine is an unstable, often mystical, and wholly inadequate tool by which to define a movement. "To repent of sins," "to trust in Jesus for salvation," "to be born again"—the expressions used by evangelicals to describe conversion imply doctrinal content. But if there is no consensus about what repentance means or why it is necessary, about what constitutes sin or a sinful nature, about who Jesus was and is, about what

Jesus did and does, and about what terms like "born again" mean, then the problem of a lack of doctrinal coherence stubbornly remains. Experience without content—or experience about which there is no agreement on the meaning of the words used to describe it—remains incapable of providing any clear identity for evangelicalism.

INSTITUTIONS AND ORGANIZATIONS

It seems the Bebbington quadrilateral is increasingly less useful in understanding evangelicalism today, whatever strengths the definition may retain for historical analysis. Nowadays, evangelicalism is so diverse that its identity cannot be discovered in shared doctrine or experience, apart from what little can be stated about its members negatively (as in, evangelicals are not Catholic and not mainline).[5] Instead, the most accurate way to define evangelicalism may be through its institutions and organizations.

To be an evangelical in this understanding is to be connected in some way to an interrelated network of seminaries, liberal arts colleges, publishers, and other parachurch groups (including the Gospel Coalition, InterVarsity Christian Fellowship, Moody Bible Institute, Wheaton College, the Evangelical Theological Society, *Christianity Today*, Crossway Books, Baker Publishing, and so on). Seen thus, evangelicalism becomes more of a social, cultural, or even marketing term than a theological one—the only time problems arise in this understanding is when the term "evangelical" is used as if it has doctrinal meaning, when in fact it does not.

A NEW, INSTITUTIONAL EVANGELICALISM

If the Bebbington quadrilateral points toward a historic evangelicalism with minimal or ill-defined doctrinal content, then the new, institutional evangelicalism is even less theologically grounded. The old definition attempted to hold together some level of doctrine (biblicism, crucicentrism) with experience (conversionism) and activism (particularly evangelism). Yet the latter two areas of experience and activism ultimately won out at the expense of theology. One can see anecdotal evidence of this throughout evangelicalism's history. For example, Charles Hodge regarded the piety of the great liberal theologian Friedrich Schleiermacher—particularly his practice of singing hymns with his family—as clear evidence of true Christian faith. More recently, I read an online discussion between a student and a scholar who was advocating critical views of the biblical text; the professor defended his self-designation as an evangelical on the grounds that he still prayed with his children every night. In both cases, piety won out over doctrinal commitment as an indicator of evangelical identity.[6]

Institutionally defined evangelicalism faces a similar problem. Clearly, there are powerful non-doctrinal forces that shape evangelical institutions and organizations, and these forces can be antithetical to clear and detailed doctrinal identities. Consider a magazine like *Christianity Today*. The success of this publication depends in part on its ability to cover costs, which is predicated on maintaining a sufficiently large readership to generate income from subscriptions and advertising. Indeed, readers and advertisers are symbiotically connected. It is not simply the case that the magazine advertises what its readership wants; what it advertises both reflects what readers want to buy and influences their buying habits. Thus, we can identify at least two factors—the need to reach a large enough reading audience and the need to reach enough advertisers—that inevitably shape the magazine's editorial policy. Neither factor naturally lends itself to exclusion and narrow boundary drawing.

The same issue confronts other evangelical institutions. Niche marketing and clear doctrinal identity are in no way antithetical: Certain Reformed, Brethren, Baptist, Presbyterian, Pentecostal, and dispensational seminaries possess clear doctrinal identities. But niche marketing has its limitations; an institution cannot become a really big beast in the evangelical world if it majors too strongly on doctrinal or ecclesiastical distinctives. Schools like Fuller and Wheaton have avoided narrow theological statements and built their sizes around generic evangelical identities and generous readings of the doctrinal bases they do have. Other schools, such as Trinity Evangelical Divinity School and Dallas Theological Seminary, have in recent years downplayed their historic distinctives, particularly in the area of eschatology.

Mass movements are formed by coalitions, and in the parachurch arena as in politics, coalitions are formed by setting aside some particulars in order to establish a popular front. Thus, the largest evangelical umbrella groups that aspire to pack a punch in their respective realms—organizations such as the ETS, the National Association of Evangelicals, and Focus on the Family—have carved out market identities without precise doctrinal measures.

BOUNDARY LINES AND OUR CULTURAL MOMENT

Whether due to a focus on religious experience, the nature of coalitions, market forces, or, indeed, a synthesis of some or all of the above, evangelicalism appears virtually impossible to define any longer by specific doctrinal commitments. In one sense, this does not concern me at all. I consider myself a Christian first, a Protestant second, and a minister in the Orthodox Presbyterian Church third. When asked if I am an evangelical, I generally respond with a question: What exactly do you mean by that term? In a world in which everyone from Joel Osteen to Brian McLaren to John MacArthur may be called an evangelical, I want to know into what pigeonhole my answer will place me.

The implications of evangelicalism's lack of definition are manifold. As a common-sense, empirical sort of person, I am left to wonder about conferences and books that discuss the future of evangelicalism or its relationship to various subjects (Barthianism, culture, Catholicism, etc.). Without a clear definition, how can evangelicalism be studied in connection with phenomena that are, comparatively speaking, much easier to identify and analyze? Furthermore, if evangelicalism has no substantive existence in the present but is merely an oft-used term, then how can it have a future worth speaking of?

More importantly, evangelicalism's lack of definition makes the drawing of boundary lines very difficult, if not impossible. Given that orthodox doctrine has provided a set of basic boundary lines for Christianity since biblical times, the lack of a clear theological identity for evangelicalism means that, whatever boundaries are drawn, they are probably not typical of historic Christianity. It is worth noting that this state of affairs comports nicely with our cultural moment. Doctrines seem to imply propositional truth claims, after all, and such claims have become passé in many quarters. Boundaries are meant to exclude, and if contemporary Western culture hates one thing above all else, it is the notion of exclusion.

BATTLES OVER BOUNDARIES

Ironically, the minimal doctrinal confessions of some evangelical institutions can exacerbate, rather than mitigate, the problem of boundary drawing. In 2004 a storm of protest followed when former Wheaton College president Duane Litfin did not renew the contract of a Wheaton faculty member who had converted to Catholicism. The faculty member claimed that he could still sign the institution's doctrinal basis in good conscience. In 2007 Baylor scholar Francis Beckwith resigned from the Evangelical Theological Society when he too left for Rome. Yet belief in inerrancy and the Trinity, the ETS's two doctrinal criteria, are entirely compatible with Roman Catholicism, while individuals with less orthodox beliefs than Beckwith, such as open theists, have been allowed to remain within the ETS.

Such examples highlight the difficulty of drawing boundaries in a movement where doctrinal bases are minimal or vague, and where an instinctive understanding of what constitutes an evangelical is generally assumed. Sadly, the individuals excluded above both had a legitimate claim to being mistreated: They were in effect held accountable to a hidden confession behind the written confession rather than to a clearly stated public standard, the meaning of which was open to scrutiny and discussion.

Admittedly, there are good historical reasons for the wider cultural fear of boundaries. The exclusion of Jews in Germany, segregation in the American South, and apartheid in South Africa all led to great evil. Exclusion has often been based on bigotry and used as a means of control, manipulation, and worse. Seen in this light, an ill-defined evangelicalism is in tune with the cultural moment, more kind and gentle and tasteful than an exclusive movement.

However, the cultural distaste for boundaries is also connected to the cultural distaste for truth claims. Such claims necessarily exclude, and in a world where the "it just feels right to me" mentality of the *Oprah Winfrey Show* is more acceptable than the authoritative "Thus says the Lord!" of Old Testament prophets, affinities between the cultural mind-set and the nebulous doctrine of much of evangelicalism are clear. Some evangelical theologians now argue for a communitarian notion of truth, where doctrinal claims are regarded as true only in a local sense, inasmuch as they can be agreed upon and applied to a given community. Others, even more skeptical, seem to root whatever remaining notions of truth they have either in practice (praxis) or process.[7]

"CONVERSATION," THEOLOGY, AND DRAWING BOUNDARIES

An interesting and related development has been the growing enthusiasm for "conversation" in recent years. Conversations are wonderful as small talk or as discussions to clarify respective positions (though "dialogue" may be a better term, perhaps).

However, when conversation rather than content becomes what is truly important, something critical is lost. Thus, as theology becomes a "conversation," traditional notions of truth face the danger of assuming less importance than mere aesthetics or modes of discourse. Indeed, doctrinal indifferentism can creep forward in a way that ends only with the sidelining or even repudiation of orthodoxy in any meaningful sense. Such a "conversational" approach to theology can find a welcome home within a movement where doctrinal boundaries are few, far between, and often equivocal.

For many evangelicals, boundary drawing and theological enforcement have come to be seen as offensive and fundamentally unchristian. My own institution, Westminster Theological Seminary, faced howls of disapproval from within and without when it addressed the writings of an Old Testament professor whom some thought had wandered outside the bounds of his faculty vow to the Westminster Standards. As a church confession, the Westminster Standards are far more elaborate than any evangelical doctrinal statement; what was interesting was not that the Standards were vague or unclear, but that holding a professor to a voluntary vow was deemed offensive by so many. Cries for academic freedom and, more bizarrely, appeals to the First Amendment of the Constitution—which limits government power, not the power of private bodies—abounded.

What drove the protests was less a belief that the professor's writings were within the bounds of Westminster orthodoxy and more a commitment to a kind of Christianity that, while not rejecting exclusive truth claims, certainly regarded exclusionary action on the basis of such claims as tasteless and to be avoided. Those in the Reformed fringe have no monopoly on such struggles, either: The open theism battles within the ETS revealed a collective unwillingness to take decisive, exclusionary action over clear digressions from historic orthodoxy. Neither the doctrinal statement of the organization nor the personal constitution of various members were, apparently, up to dealing with heterodoxy. From the time of Paul, the church has drawn boundaries. Such has been considered necessary for her well-being and even her survival. A movement that cannot or will not draw boundaries, or that allows the modern cultural fear of exclusion to set its theological agenda, is doomed to lose its doctrinal identity. Once it does, it will drift from whatever moorings it may have had in historic Christianity.

NOTES

1. See David W. Bebbington, *Evangelicalism in Modern Britain: A History from the 1730s to the 1980s* (London: Unwin Hyman, 1989). A good collection of essays interacting with Bebbington's proposals is Michael A. G. Haykin and Kenneth J. Stewart, eds., *The Emergence of Evangelicalism: Exploring Historical Continuities* (Nottingham, U.K.: Apollos, 2008).

2. A Catholic might argue at this point that this problem has been part of Protestantism from the start: abandon the teaching magisterium of Rome, and you are left with nothing to stop the multiplication of sects. Such criticism is valid perhaps when it comes to the hostile application of labels (as in a Catholic writer lumping both Calvin and Servetus together as "Protestant"), but I am here thinking of self-conscious identity. I think of myself as Presbyterian: I can point to a certain set of doctrinal standards and ecclesiastical principles that define the term. An Anabaptist can do the same with her church, as can a Baptist or a Methodist. We each know our distinctive histories and doctrines. This is not the case with the rather nebulous concept that is evangelicalism.

3. "The Bible alone, and the Bible in its entirety, is the Word of God written and is therefore inerrant in the autographs. God is a Trinity, Father, Son, and Holy Spirit, each an uncreated person, one in essence, equal in power and glory." http://www.etsjets.org/about.

4. These affirmations are embodied in the Cambridge Declaration: http://www.
alliancenet.org/partner/Article_Display_Page/0..PTID307086_CHID798774
_CIID1411364.00.html.

5. In the wider culture, even these exclusions are now negotiable: In 2005, *Time* listed Father Richard John Neuhaus, the well-known Catholic intellectual, as one of North America's 25 most influential evangelicals. The list also included Rick Warren, Brian McLaren, and J.I. Packer, indicating pre-

cisely the irrelevance of significant doctrinal criteria for being designated an evangelical. http://www.time.com/time/covers/1101050207/index.html.

6. Hodge's comment reads as follows: "When in Berlin the writer often attended Schleiermacher's church. The hymns to be sung were printed on slips of paper and distributed at the door. They were always evangelical and spiritual to an eminent degree, filled with praise and gratitude to the Redeemer. Tholuck said that Schleiermacher, when sitting in the evening with his family, would often say, 'Hush, children; let us sing a hymn of praise to Christ.' Can we doubt that he is singing those praises now? To whomsoever Christ is God, St. John assures us, Christ is a Saviour." *Systematic Theology* (Grand Rapids: Eerdmans, 1979), II, 440.

7. See, for example, John R. Franke, *Manifold Witness* (Nashville: Abingdon, 2009); Brian D. McLaren, *A New Kind of Christianity* (New York: HarperOne, 2010).

CHAPTER TWO

Exclusion and the Evangelical Mind

No one likes to be excluded, set on the periphery. Some evangelical academics, aware of this, desire not to exclude anyone who thinks that the Bible is a jolly good book and that Jesus was a decent bloke (to borrow some phrases from my homeland). Similarly they desire not to be excluded themselves from mainstream scholarly culture.

Yet the conservative scholar often faces criticisms, even as the liberal receives commendation. Numerous examples come to mind. Take, for instance, the familiar and tiresome figure of the social-climbing evangelical academic who never misses a chance to trash anybody who happens to stand just to his right theologically—as in, "Dr. Z. is an idiot for believing in an early date for Daniel" (or Pauline authorship of Ephesians, or inerrancy, or whatever the issue may be). At the same time, this academic always finds something of value in, and even fawns over, those to his left. Usually, his appreciation is preceded by a throat-clearing comment: "Of course,

I disagree with Professor X on Subject A" (his rejection of biblical authority, perhaps, or his denial of the resurrection, or his dismissal of the doctrine of the Trinity). Such a disavowal is quickly followed by affirmation of an area of agreement: "But I really do find his work on Subject B (reader response theory, or Johannine studies, or Second Temple Judaism) to be extremely helpful." The evangelical scholar's assessments may be quite correct; my point here is simply to highlight the cultural mind-set his pattern of speech reveals.

I certainly do not intend to belittle good arguments and scholarship, wherever they are to be found, nor to prop up poor work produced by theological conservatives. Yet as an evangelical academic myself, I find it interesting to note the way in which, with some writers, the perceived faults of more conservative authors are denounced with bombastic rhetoric, while the blasphemies and heresies of those on the left are dismissed with a casual wave of the academic hand. Isn't what's good for the conservative goose also good for liberal gander? In addition, what does such behavior say about who such evangelical academics perceive as true enemies of the faith? Is all boundary drawing tasteless—except when applied against those more conservative than the one drawing the boundary?

A similar mind-set may be observed in the tendency to invite an increasingly broad range of speakers to evangelical conferences. Again, to be clear: I am not criticizing the practice of speaking with non-evangelicals at conferences. I do it myself. Nor am I criticizing the practice of inviting speakers to evangelical colleges and seminaries who cannot sign the doctrinal bases required of resident faculty. I have hosted a Roman Catholic friend at Westminster Theological Seminary, and I have lectured at liberal institutions. I am not pleading for cultural isolationism or obscurantism. However, the context in which such speaking occurs is crucial. If the context seems to indicate that the breadth of views expressed by the speakers falls within the bounds of evangelicalism, then my point that evangelicalism has, practically speaking, no doctrinal definition is further reinforced. A lecture series or conference held in honor of an evangelical leader might fall under this category of events that, contextually, attendees could reasonably expect to be thoroughly evangelical. In the area of publishing, certain book awards could fall under the same category.

SENDING EQUIVOCAL SIGNALS

Inviting speakers who equivocate on, say, homosexuality or universalism or the authority of Scripture is increasingly common at evangelical conferences and lecture series, as are invitations for such thinkers to publish with houses that have historic evangelical reputations. Granted, the evangelical conference looks more respectable, polite, and mainstream with the inclusion of a diversified speakers' panel, and the Christian publisher lands a big-name author with strong sales potential. Yet a highly equivocal signal is sent to students, churches, and church members about evangelical orthodoxy.

If evangelicalism has no boundaries, then no boundaries have been transgressed, of course. But let us be more honest about the vacuous nature of evangelical theological identity. Is contemporary evangelicalism indeed impossible to define doctrinally? Is it merely a sociological category, loosely bounded by a wide range of institutions and organizations? In that case, evangelical theology becomes not an outgrowth of historic doctrinal concerns but rather whatever theology is currently taught at evangelical seminaries, editorialized in evangelical magazines, and published by evangelical presses—and let us not pretend otherwise.

THE CHALLENGE TO MORALITY

Lacking a strong doctrinal center, evangelicalism's coherence as a coalition of institutions and organizations is about to come under huge strain—a strain that I believe will render the coalition unsustainable in days ahead.

The most pressing challenge from the wider culture is the ethical matter of homosexuality. Cultural attitudes have changed quickly on homosexuality. I remember saying at a Bible study just fifteen years ago that the gay rights movement had reached its high-water mark; for most people, I opined, homosexuality was so obviously immoral that general consensus could not be overcome. I now list that statement as among the most boneheaded and short-sighted I have ever made—and the competition in that sphere is more than a little fierce. I had not reckoned with the power of gay-friendly media presentations, nor with the way the rising generation's lack of moral foundations could be easily exploited. A Pew Forum survey in 2009 found that the vast majority of Americans under age thirty no longer view gay marriage as an issue at all.[1]

A few years after my Bible study misstatement, as the sobering pace of the gay-rights agenda's advancement began to dawn on me, I told a senior colleague and respected evangelical biblical scholar at Aberdeen University that evangelicals were likely to start equivocating on homosexuality. Nonsense, he declared; that could never happen. I believe he was as naïve then as I had been several years earlier.

Those pastors who have remained strong in upholding a biblical position against homosexual behavior increasingly face consequences. Consider the reaction to President Barack Obama's decision a couple of years ago to ask evangelical Rick Warren to pray at his inauguration. The political left exploded in outrage that someone who had supported Proposition 8 (the banning of gay marriage in California) would be asked to participate in the event. Regardless of what one might think of Warren's theology, his church had been deeply involved in various social issues (including AIDS, the development of clean water sources for developing nations, and support for orphans and abused children) generally embraced by the left.[2] Yet this work counted for nothing in the context of his opposition to gay marriage. Opposing homosexuality was becoming something akin to an unforgivable sin, as offensive to many as being a white supremacist or a child pornographer.

The impact of this wider cultural shift on evangelical institutions and organizations will be dramatic. Those who aspire to an elusive "place at the cultural table" will find themselves between a rock and hard place. A college will not, for example, be able to oppose homosexuality and still be regarded as the evangelical Harvard. A speaker will not be able to criticize gay culture and still be treated by mainstream media as an intelligent commentator on the wider world. Scholars can forget offering papers at academic conferences in which they argue, with any degree of sympathy, that the Bible condemns homosexual practice—this will be classified as "hate speech" and typically be rejected at scholarly gatherings.

THE DRIVE FOR TOTAL
ACCEPTANCE OF HOMOSEXUALITY

Any readers skeptical of this line of thinking as fear-mongering might reflect on an example from 1995. The press excoriated R. Albert Mohler Jr., the president of Southern Baptist Theological Seminary, that year for delivering a paper where he highlighted homosexuality as symptomatic of the West's moral decay. Editorial writers were furious, describing him as promoting "compassionate hatred" and persecution of homosexuals. That was sixteen years ago, long before gay marriage was becoming legally acceptable and vacuous figures like Perez Hilton were considered remotely credible. Today's world is far more tolerant of homosexuality; we can expect reactions to any criticism of it to be at least as aggressive.[3]

Indeed, while there are complexities and nuances in the homosexual debate, it is doubtful that the wider world will grant any space for such. Those driving hard for complete and total acceptance of homosexuality are not in the mood for negotiating compromises. Why should they be? The cultural tide is flowing irresistibly in their favor. Attempts by social conservatives at nuance (from the typical "hate the sin, love the sinner" language to fine parsing of where exactly someone who feels same-sex attraction crosses the line into sin) will be seen as duplicitous. Do evangelical leaders and institutions grant the legitimacy of homosexuality or not? Yes or no? Only a one-word answer will suffice. All Christians, evangelical and otherwise, will face the question, and their answer to it will determine whether they have credibility in the wider culture.

Further, if academic accreditation agencies in the United States go with the cultural flow, then accreditation standards may well come to include benchmarks on sexuality that require acceptance of homosexuality. Such a change would be challenged in the courts on freedom of religion grounds, but I would not expect an outcome favorable to traditional Christianity.[4]

Predictably, there will be no evangelical consensus on homosexuality because ethical consideration of it rests upon theological categories of biblical authority, creation, fall, Christology, redemption, and consummation—and there is no evangelical consensus in any of these areas. With evangelicalism no longer defined by doctrinal commitments, there can and will be no evangelical consensus on homosexuality. Marry this theological vagary to a strong desire for a place at the cultural table, and greater acceptance of homosexuality among evangelicals is all but assured.[5]

THE CHALLENGE TO AUTHORITY

The challenge to sexual morality leads directly to a challenge to biblical authority. If evangelicals are going to reject the legitimacy of homosexuality for any reason other than anti-gay bigotry, it can only be on the basis of what the Bible actually teaches—and that must rest upon both a shared understanding of scriptural authority and a consistently biblical hermeneutic. Yet scriptural authority and hermeneutics have been highly contested within evangelical institutions and organizations over the last decades, without widespread agreement on either.

It is not hard to find evidence that biblical authority is being eroded or, at the very least, changed. Within some churches, preaching and reading of the Bible is increasingly less common. Indeed, preaching as proclamation has been replaced by conversational discussions of biblical themes in some congregations, or even supplanted in favor of drama and dance. In making this observation, I am not primarily issuing a judgment but rather observing a shift in church life that rests ultimately upon a changed understanding of the nature and function of Scripture.

Within academia, scholars who consider themselves evangelicals increasingly reject biblical inerrancy. Of course, while evangelicals have always held a high view of Scripture's authority, it is arguable that inerrancy was never the universal position for evangelicalism as a whole. Nor was there ever a single understanding of what inerrancy meant, even by those who subscribed to the doctrine. One has only to look to the position on Scripture of a man like James Denney in the nineteenth century or to the diverse makeup of the present membership of ETS to see the diversity within evangelicalism. However, at present evangelical views of Scripture and interpretation are so divergent as to defy any claims to coherence within the movement.

IS BIBLICAL AUTHORITY INTELLECTUALLY VIABLE?

Part of the problem is that traditional, orthodox notions of biblical authority have become an embarrassment to many in the evangelical world. Such notions are incompatible with the presuppositions, methods, and epistemologies of the secular academy and thus are no longer intellectually viable. In recent years a number of faculty members at evangelical institutions have written books for evangelical presses that attempt to revise or reject major parts of the traditional view of Scripture.

These critiques follow two basic approaches, neither exclusive of the other. First, there is the historical-critical approach, which sees the textual history of the Bible, its internal contradictions, and evidence from external literary and archaeological sources as rendering the doctrine of inerrancy (and possibly also a conservative view of scriptural authority in general) unsustainable. Second, there is the epistemological approach that focuses on hermeneutical issues. Informed by various critical epistemologies, some evangelical theologians have recast biblical interpretation as a community's response to the written text, shifting away from older notions of objective truth. When the two approaches combine, the historical-critical and the epistemological, one is left wondering whether God has revealed Himself in a way that can be meaningfully known.

I do not have space here to analyze these approaches. Instead, I want only to highlight the fact that both critiques render evangelicalism increasingly equivocal on traditional Christian doctrines and ethics. Indeed, if homosexuality is the clear point of challenge in the area of ethics, then my guess is that the historicity and individuality of Adam will become the clear point of challenge to scriptural authority. For Adam is crucial: Speaking in the terms of my own tradition, if there were no historical Adam and no fall, then the entire system of doctrine outlined in the Westminster Standards would collapse. More importantly—and beyond the confines of Reformed theology—Paul's statements about Adam in Romans 5 and 1 Corinthians 15 are crucial to interpreting Pauline theology and the gospel itself. The doctrine of all Christians, not just Presbyterians, is vitally connected to Adam.[6]

HOMOSEXUALITY,
A REAL ADAM, AND EVOLUTION

In the wider culture, the aggressiveness with which various theories of evolution are being promulgated indicates that, like homosexuality, it is a matter on which dissenters will soon be treated as members of a lunatic fringe. Within Christian circles, groups like the BioLogos Forum exist to promote acceptance of evolution. While it is true that BioLogos's position on the historical Adam is somewhat less defined than its stand on evolution—contributing scholar Bruce Waltke, for example, holds both to evolution and the historical Adam—it is likely that the position of writers such as Waltke will come to be regarded by the wider secular world as an attempt to cling to the vestiges of orthodoxy by an unsubstantiated act of will.

Secular critics are probably correct to see the marriage of evolutionary theory with belief in a historical Adam as incoherent. Of more concern for this essay, however, are the implications for evangelicalism. As with homosexuality, crucial decisions will have to be made, particularly: Do we want to be culturally credible, and how much ground are we willing to surrender in order to do so? Cultural relevance can be a cruel mistress. In my own field of history, there are scholars who will always regard me as at worst mediocre, at best inconsistent, because I believe in the resurrection, something that defies verification by standard historical procedure. Do I abandon this doctrine for a precious seat at the high table of the historical guild?

During a time when you cannot have your cake of social credibility and eat it too, where do evangelical institutions and organizations place themselves on issues like homosexuality and the historical Adam? More significantly, do our institutions and organizations have the theological foundation for doing anything besides either going with the cultural flow or maintaining traditional positions through sheer will power and perceived bigotry? Institutions and individuals that have moved away from a high understanding of biblical authority will find it impossible to avoid the former without being guilty of the latter.

Still more worrisome: While we labor under the illusion that there continues to be something called "evangelicalism," confusing signals will come from the various corners that claim to represent the movement, and these will have disturbing pastoral consequences. A friend reported to me last year that the presence of a certain speaker at a certain conference led his ministerial colleague to assume that this speaker's teaching was compatible with orthodoxy. That is not a safe assumption, but it is one to which people might be led, given the lay understanding that evangelicalism carries within it the essence of Christian orthodoxy. The persistence of the term "evangelicalism" is therefore a matter of pastoral concern, even before it is a matter of ecclesiastical or academic concern.

NOTES

1. "Majority Continues to Support Civil Unions" 9 October, 2009; at http://pewforum.org/Gay-Marriage-and-Homosexuality/Majority-Continues-To-Support-Civil-Unions.aspx.

2. Saddleback Church's various social causes are listed at http://www.saddleback.com/giving/.

3. Gregory A. Wills, *Southern Baptist Theological Seminary, 1859–2009* (Oxford, England: Oxford Univ. Press, 2009), 543-44.

4. Such a call for change has already been made to ATS: See the report "Sex and the Seminary," available at http://www.religiousinstitute.org/research-report/sex-and-the-seminary-preparing-ministers-for-sexual-health-and-justice.

5. A good analysis of what is at stake in this debate for evangelicals is Denny Burk's article, "Why Evangelicals Should Ignore Brian McLaren: How the New Testament Requires Evangelicals to Render a Judgment on the Moral Status of Homosexuality," in *Themelios* 35.2 (July, 2010), 212–26. Available for download at http://thegospelcoalition.org/publications.

6. Michael Reeves's article, "Adam and Eve," is an excellent and accessible summary of what is theologically at stake in the debates about the historicity of Adam. It is available at http://www.reformation21.org/articles/adam-and-eve.php.

CHAPTER THREE

The Real Scandal of the Evangelical Mind

When Mark Noll declared that the scandal of the evangelical mind was that there was no mind, he meant to criticize the lack of cultural and theological engagement among evangelicals. I agree there is a scandal involving the evangelical mind, though I understand the problem in the exact opposite way. It is not that there is no mind, but rather that there is no evangelical.

As with the urban spaceman in the Bonzo Dog Doo-Dah Band song, evangelicalism has a twist: It doesn't exist. There may be various sectarian "evangelicalisms"—conservative, confessional, Anabaptist, Wesleyan, Pentecostal, open, and so on—but these are not variations of a single melody so much as different songs altogether. As stand-alone traditions, they may share some common ground with each other, but not necessarily more ground than they share with other, non-evangelical streams of Christianity. There simply is no pure, platonic ideal of evangelicalism, no common identity in which all evangelicalisms participate.

CHRISTIANITY VIEWED AS A CULT

Furthermore, the pressures on institutions and organizations that identify as evangelical are sure to change those institutions ahead. It seems inevitable that organizations will become either more narrow and sectarian or more mainstream and secular, which will lead to fundamental realignments within the evangelical world. Those institutions that cherish their place at the cultural table will have to accept the legitimacy of homosexual relationships and to abandon a fully Pauline gospel of salvation predicated on a historical Adam. Those institutions wishing to maintain traditional orthodoxy on these points will have to accept their status as marginal figures in the broader world, objects of scorn and not serious contributors to the public square.

As so many on the left of the evangelical spectrum observe, Christendom is over. What many fail to mention is that the death of Christendom also leads to the social perception that orthodox Christianity is a kind of cult. Thus it was in Imperial Rome; thus will it be again in the twenty-first-century West.

It is likely that the coming cultural storms will be best weathered by evangelical organizations and institutions with more precisely defined doctrinal statements, particularly statements that are close to, or identical with, historic creeds and confessions. The last one hundred years of evangelicalism has shown that minimal doctrinal bases do not provide real resistance to heterodoxy and the downgrading of doctrine. Of course, no creed can safeguard orthodoxy alone; fidelity and integrity on the part of leaders and gatekeepers are also required. But without a strong and complete doctrinal confession, gatekeeping becomes nearly impossible, even for well-intentioned and faithful leaders.

GRASPING THE BASIC ELEMENTS OF THE FAITH

The scenario I outline here will likely sound despairing to those who have been inspired by Mark Noll's vision for a culturally engaged evangelicalism. After all, without an evangelicalism (singular) of which one can predicate a mind, there is no hope for a seat at the coveted cultural table. Certainly, my scenario is not particularly attractive: Who among us wants to become less important, more marginal, and increasingly despised?

Yet as attractive as Noll's vision was, it always struck me as somewhat professorial, more likely to resonate with the middle-class evangelical intelligentsia in, say, Wheaton, Illinois, than with the typical Christian in a typical church across the country. If the church as a whole is losing its ability to be "salt and light" in the culture, it is not because its members have no opinion of the films of Bernardo Bertolucci, no appreciation for the poetry of Emily Dickinson, and no regular slot on *The Charlie Rose Show*. More likely, it is because they do not have a solid grasp of the basic elements of the faith, as taught in Scripture and affirmed by the confessions and catechisms of the church.

One reason for this lack is the decision by many Christians to identify more strongly with the coalition movement of evangelicalism than with a particular denomination or local church. Even if we grant contemporary evangelicalism a minimal doctrinal identity, its most passionate supporters would still acknowledge that the nature of a coalition sidelines doctrinal distinctives. The result is to subtly diminish large swathes of biblical teaching of their importance, an outcome that bleeds into churches and shapes the mind-sets of pastors and laypeople alike, setting low expectations for doctrinal knowledge. As evangelicalism loses even the minimal doctrinal content it once possessed, so, too, churches that identify with it will be further diminished doctrinally.[1]

I do not mean to imply that I question the faith of believers with whom I might disagree on, for instance, the mode and subjects of baptism. But I do mean to say that the issue of baptism is important enough that one ought to have an opinion on it. Yet as long as Christians find their primary identity in a nebulous, ill-defined evangelicalism to which everyone from five-point Calvinists to open theists may belong, then such matters as baptism, the Lord's Supper, and ecclesiology will be necessarily sidelined or even watered down as not worthy of dividing over—as will, increasingly, views on justification, sanctification, the doctrine of God, and ethical issues like homosexuality. No wonder some evangelicals have thrown up their hands in despair and returned to Rome. Evangelicalism today simply does not provide the authority and identity of the Roman Catholic Church, and the situation looks to become worse ahead.[2]

A NEW SECTARIANISM

Yet there may be a bright side to evangelicalism's decline. When the fog has lifted and it becomes clear that all talk of evangelicalism as a clearly defined movement was a category mistake—a confusion of a coalition for a doctrinally committed movement—then new alliances may emerge. The days of being considered part of an evangelicalism that regarded Calvinists and Anabaptists as closer to each other than, say, orthodox Dominicans and open theists, respectively, may come to an end. Surprisingly, this development could lower the polemical temperature in some quarters: Once various groups are no longer competing for ownership of the evangelical brand, they might be able to assess one another in a less defensive manner.[3] Looked at from this angle, the new sectarianism may open the door to fresh dialogue across old party lines, dialogue that can be honest and principled because everybody knows where everyone else stands from the start, with no false assumptions about falling under the same ecclesiastical umbrella. Wouldn't this arrangement better fit an era in which differences are respected and diversity is celebrated?

Regardless of whether the scenario I have outlined comes about, it is clear that the cultural referee is about to call time out on evangelicals and evangelicalism, if not on traditional religions entirely.

No evangelical leader or organization can prevent it. The gay lobby, militant secularists, and atheists who deride any religious belief as distasteful will force Christians either into capitulation to their demands or a sectarianism that thrusts us to the margins. Abandoning the myth of the evangelical movement can only help us, as it will free us to be who we truly are and to speak the gospel in all of its richness as we understand it. This is what our day and generation needs.

The real scandal of the evangelical mind currently is not that it lacks a mind, but that it lacks any agreed-upon evangel. Until we acknowledge that this is the case—until we can agree on what exactly it is that constitutes the evangel—all talk about evangelicalism as a real, coherent movement is likely to be little more than a chimera, or a trick with smoke and mirrors.

NOTES

1. As one friend once said to me, based on his years of pastoral experience, a church's stated confessional or doctrinal standards represent the high point of knowledge that can ever be expected from a typical church member. Put bluntly, if it is not in the standards, the members will, on the whole, not regard it as important. Thus, to take your ecclesiastical or personal cue on doctrine from broad evangelical organizations and institutions is virtually to guarantee mediocrity in overall doctrinal literacy.

2. I make this point in more detail in my review of Mark A. Noll and Carolyn Nystrom, *Is the Reformation Over?* (Grand Rapids: Baker, 2005), available at http://www.reformation21.org/shelf-life/is-the-reformation-over.php. The review was later cited by Francis Beckwith on this very point—that evangelicalism now no longer provides people with sufficient reason not to be Roman Catholics—as being a watershed in his own decision to return to Rome. See Francis J. Beckwith, *Return to Rome: Confessions of an Evangelical Catholic* (Grand Rapids: Brazos, 2008), 83.

3. Hopefully, we will also have no further use for silly questions such as "Was Bonhoeffer an evangelical?" Frankly, who cares? The important question is surely not about which present-day party can lay claim to him but something more like: "What can Bonhoeffer's life, teaching, and death tell me about how to believe and live—and die—as a Christian?"

THE MAKING OF AN ATHEIST

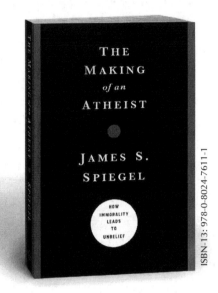

ISBN-13: 978-0-8024-7611-1

How did such folks as Richard Dawkins, Sam Harris, Daniel Dennett, and Christopher Hitchens become such ardent atheists? If we are to believe them there are not enough rational grounds for belief in God. But is this the whole story? Could it be that their opposition to religious faith has more to do with passion than reason? What if, in the end, evidence has little to do with how atheists arrive at their anti-faith?

For the atheist, the missing ingredient is not evidence but obedience. The psalmist declares, "The fool says in his heart there is no God" (Psalm 14:1), and in the book of Romans, Paul makes it clear that lack of evidence is not the atheist's problem. *The Making of an Atheist* confirms these biblical truths and describes the moral and psychological dynamics involved in the abandonment of faith.

MOODY
Publishers™

From the Word to Life

moodypublishers.com

CITY OF MAN

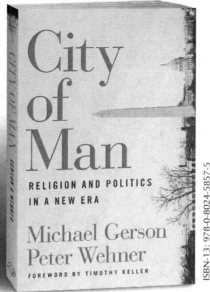

ISBN-13: 978-0-8024-5857-5

An era has ended. The political expression that most galvanized evangelicals during the past quarter-century, the Religious Right, is fading. What's ahead is unclear. Millions of faith-based voters still exist, and they continue to care deeply about hot-button issues like abortion and gay marriage, but the shape of their future political engagement remains to be formed.

Into this uncertainty, former White House insiders Michael Gerson and Peter Wehner seek to call evangelicals toward a new kind of political engagement—a kind that is better both for the church and the country, a kind that cannot be co-opted by either political party, a kind that avoids the historic mistakes of both the Religious Left and the Religious Right.

MOODY
Publishers™

From the Word to Life

moodypublishers.com